Be

The story of Noah is found
in the Old Testament of the Bible,
in chapters VI to IX of Genesis.

The text of this book
has been prepared with reference to:
The Good News Bible (1994),
The New English Bible (1970),
The New Jerusalem Bible (1990),
The Revised Standard Version (1973).

Series editor: Jacqueline Vallon

*The publishers wish to thank
Geoffrey Marshall-Taylor, Educational Consultant,
for his kind help.*

ISBN 1 85103 267 3
© 1997, Gallimard Jeunesse
Illustrations coloured by Anne Gutman
English text © 1998, Moonlight Publishing Ltd
First published in the United Kingdom 1998
by Moonlight Publishing Ltd, 36 Stratford Road, London W8
Printed in Italy by Editoriale Libraria

Best Bible Stories

THE STORY OF NOAH

Retold by Clare Best
Illustrated by Maurice Pommier

Moonlight Publishing

The world was full of violence and people led wicked lives. When God saw this he felt miserable. What had become of his wondrous creation, his world of beauty and harmony? He had made people to be like himself and had given them all they needed – plants to

eat, animals to look after. He had
planned a place where his creatures
could live in happiness and peace.
The problem started with Cain. He was
the son of Adam and Eve, the first man
and the first woman. Cain grew jealous
of his younger brother Abel and killed
him. Then, as the number of people
increased, so did their wickedness.

In those days, long ago, people lived to a great age: six or seven hundred years was common. Some people lived almost a thousand years – Methuselah was 969 when he died!

Seeing how people enjoyed doing evil, God decided to shorten their lives, so that in future most people would live no more than 120 years.

But even though people lived fewer years, their wickedness kept growing. Their hearts and minds were filled with nothing but evil thoughts and plots. They were jealous, envious, vengeful and spiteful. They hurt and killed one another. One wicked deed would give rise to thousands of others so that evil multiplied day by day.

This evil spread until the whole of creation was spoilt, and the delicate balance of nature was upset. Everything in the world was ruined by evil.

God said, "I will destroy everything I have created, the human beings and all the creatures – the reptiles, the birds, everything, for I'm sorry I ever made them."

But Noah was different. He was a good man, honest and true. He looked to God as his guide through life. In everything he did and thought, he tried to please God.

And God thought well of Noah – there was no reason to destroy him along with all the others.

God told Noah his plan: "The world is violent because of humans. I have decided to bring an end to the whole human race, and all other living things at the same time. I will send a flood to cover the earth and destroy all life. But I will spare you and your family. Build yourself an ark out of cypress wood, to float on the waters.

Coat it with tar, inside and out, to make it waterproof. It must be 133 metres long, 22 metres wide and 13 metres high. Build three decks and divide them into rooms. Make a door in the side and put a roof over the top of the ark."

So Noah set to work with his sons Shem, Ham and Japheth, and they built the ark.
Then God said to Noah, "You will go into the ark, you and your family, and you will take with you two of each kind of animal and bird, a male and a female. This way, life on earth may one day continue. Take plenty of food for everyone. Be quick – in seven days time I will send rain for forty days

and forty nights to destroy my creation."
Noah was obedient. He did everything
exactly as God had asked him to.

Noah was 600 years old when the flood came. He and his wife, his sons and their wives went into the ark to escape the waters.

And into the ark with Noah and his family went every kind of animal and bird. Two by two they went in...
The largest mammals, the smallest insects, beasts that run, birds that fly, domestic animals, wild animals...

There was room for them all.
Then God shut the door behind Noah.
That very day, rain began to fall.

The springs of the great deep poured water, heaven's gates were opened, and the flood surged over the earth.

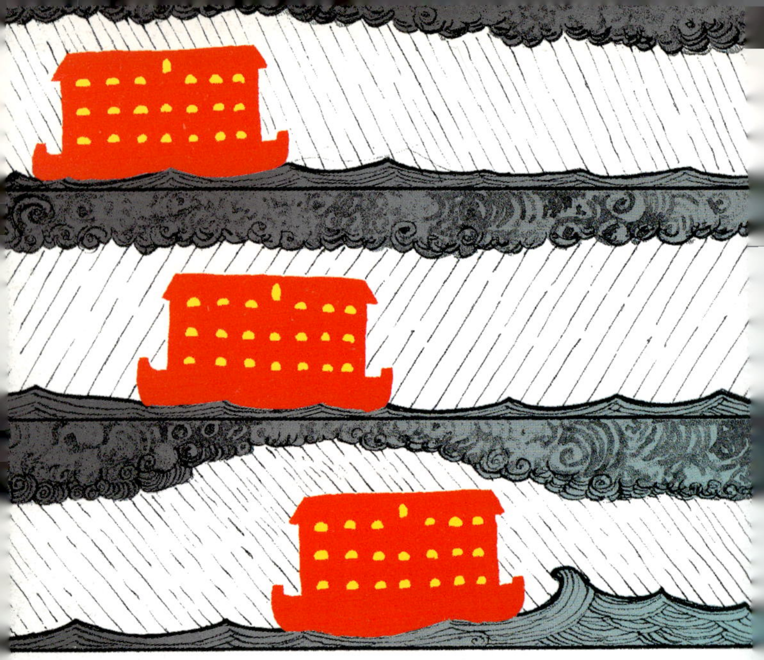

The flood became deeper and deeper, lifting the ark so that it floated on top of the water, and drifted over the surface.

Rain fell for forty days and forty nights, until even the highest mountains were under water.
The flood waters rose for a hundred and fifty days, and every living thing was wiped from the face of the earth.

But God had not forgotten Noah and all the animals in the ark. He sent a mighty wind over the earth to dry up the flood waters. He stopped the flow from the great deep and he closed heaven's gates.

The rain stopped. Little by little the flood waters went down, until Noah's ark came to rest on the summit of the first mountain to appear – Mount Ararat.

The waters kept going down, and gradually other mountain tops appeared above the water. After forty days Noah opened a window in the ark. He wanted to be sure the ground was dry before getting off the boat, so he released a raven. It flew around, unable to find a dry place to perch.

Then Noah sent out a dove, and neither could the dove find a place to land. It flew back to the ark and Noah took it in.

Noah waited seven days and then released the dove again. That evening it returned to him, carrying in its beak a fresh leaf from an olive tree.
Now Noah knew that the land was dry at last and that trees and plants must be growing again.

Noah waited seven days more, and then he let the dove fly from the ark once again. This time it did not come back to him.

God told Noah, "Leave the ark. Take your family and all the animals with you. They will breed and multiply and populate the earth."
So all the mammals and reptiles and birds left the ark, two by two, glad to be back on dry land at last!

It was important that this new life should be in tune with God, the creator. Noah decided to offer a sacrifice to God, as a way of showing thanks and respect. He found a large stone and made an altar. Then he sacrificed several animals and burned their bodies on the altar.

The smoke from the fire rose up to heaven and God was pleased when he smelled it. It carried the prayers and love of the people for their God.
God said, "Never again will I curse the earth because of what people do. I know that from childhood they can be evil, and it is difficult for them to be good. Never again will I destroy all living things as I have just done."

God blessed Noah and his family and said to them, "Have many children, so that your families and theirs will spread over all the earth. I place in your power all living creatures. As well as the green plants I gave you before, you now have animals for food too." And so people began to raise animals for meat.

God also said to them,
"Do not take human life, for people are made to be like God."

Then God reassured them:
"Now I am going to make a promise to you and your descendants, and to all the living creatures that were with you in the ark – all the birds and animals. I promise I will never again send a flood to destroy life on earth."

God went on,
"As a sign of my promise to all creation,
I am putting my bow in the clouds.
Whenever I gather clouds in the sky
and the rainbow appears, I will remember
my pact with you and all life. Every
rainbow will be a sign of the peace
I have made with you."

So life started again on earth.
Human beings made a fresh beginning, and God renewed his promise over and over again, just as he had made the pact the first time with Noah.
And what of Noah? God was good to him. He and his sons became the first farmers. He lived another 350 years.

MOONLIGHT PUBLISHING

PUBLISHERS OF MULTICULTURAL BOOKS INTRODUCING CHILDREN TO THE RELIGIONS OF THE WORLD

TALES OF HEAVEN AND EARTH

SARAH, WHO LOVED LAUGHING
A TALE FROM THE BIBLE

THE SECRETS OF KAIDARA
AN ANIMIST TALE FROM AFRICA

I WANT TO TALK TO GOD
A TALE FROM ISLAM

THE RIVER GODDESS
A TALE FROM HINDUISM

CHILDREN OF THE MOON
YANOMAMI LEGENDS

I'LL TELL YOU A STORY
TALES FROM THE JEWISH TRADITION

THE PRINCE WHO BECAME A BEGGAR
A BUDDHIST TALE

JESUS SAT DOWN AND SAID...
THE PARABLES OF JESUS

MUHAMMAD'S NIGHT JOURNEY
A TALE FROM ISLAM

ST FRANCIS, THE MAN WHO SPOKE TO BIRDS
TALES OF ST FRANCIS OF ASSISI

THE MAGIC OF CHRISTMAS
CHRISTMAS TALES FROM EUROPE

RAMA, THE HEROIC PRINCE
A HINDU TALE FROM THE RAMAYANA

WHEN BRENDAN DISCOVERED PARADISE
A CHRISTIAN TALE FROM IRELAND

Jacqueline Vallon, who devised this series, is editor of religious books for children at Gallimard Jeunesse, in France. She also has experience as a teacher of literature and French, and as a journalist specialising in world religions.

Maurice Pommier used to be a sorter with the French postal service. He taught himself to draw and has always created stories with pictures for children. But it was only when a friend insisted he show his work to a well-known Paris publisher that he embarked on his second career, as an illustrator creating and contributing to a wide variety of books for children and adults. Seen here in a self-portrait with a long, Biblical beard, he likes illustrating Bible stories because he feels that they are timeless and true.

Best Bible Stories

The stories in this collection introduce children to characters and themes that they will meet again and again in art, music and literature, and in everyday language. People have found spiritual insights in the stories for centuries.

Our *Best Bible Stories* are retold close to the original scriptures, after comparing several of the most respected translations, including *The Good News Bible* (1994), *The New English Bible* (1970), *The New Jerusalem Bible* (1990) and *The Revised Standard Version* (1973).

The aim of this series is to make the stories more accessible and attractive to children, using clear language without stylistic effects or old-fashioned expressions. Occasionally, and to avoid repetition, narrative has been simplified. Long genealogies have been cut out.

The only additions are brief explanations of key ideas – what a prophet is, why sacrifices are significant – and these are built into the text.